THE SEVEN WONDERS OF THE MODERN WORLD

PETRA

BY SARA GREEN

BELLWETHER MEDIA • MINNEAPOLIS, MN

Blastoff! Discovery launches a new mission: reading to learn. Filled with facts and features, each book offers you an exciting new world to explore!

BLASTOFF! UNIVERSE

BLASTOFF! BEGINNERS
GRADE K

BLASTOFF! READERS
GRADES 1-3

BLASTOFF! DISCOVERY
GRADE 4

This edition first published in 2021 by Bellwether Media, Inc.

No part of this publication may be reproduced in whole or in part without written permission of the publisher. For information regarding permission, write to Bellwether Media, Inc., Attention: Permissions Department, 6012 Blue Circle Drive, Minnetonka, MN 55343.

Library of Congress Cataloging-in-Publication Data

Names: Green, Sara, 1964- author.
Title: Petra / by Sara Green.
Description: Minneapolis, MN : Bellwether Media, Inc., 2021. | Series: Blastoff! discovery: The seven wonders of the modern world | Includes bibliographical references and index. | Audience: Ages 7-13 | Audience: Grades 4-6 | Summary: "Engaging images accompany information about Petra. The combination of high-interest subject matter and narrative text is intended for students in grades 3 through 8"–Provided by publisher.
Identifiers: LCCN 2020018892 (print) | LCCN 2020018893 (ebook) | ISBN 9781644872703 (library binding) | ISBN 9781681037332 (ebook)
Subjects: LCSH: Petra (Extinct city)–Juvenile literature.
Classification: LCC DS154.9.P48 G74 2021 (print) | LCC DS154.9.P48 (ebook) | DDC 939.4/8–dc23
LC record available at https://lccn.loc.gov/2020018892
LC ebook record available at https://lccn.loc.gov/2020018893

Editor: Betsy Rathburn   Designer: Brittany McIntosh

Printed in the United States of America, North Mankato, MN.

TABLE OF CONTENTS

A DESERT TREASURE	4
WHAT IS PETRA?	6
INNOVATIVE ENGINEERS	10
LOST AND FOUND	20
EXPLORE, RESTORE, AND PROTECT	24
GLOSSARY	30
TO LEARN MORE	31
INDEX	32

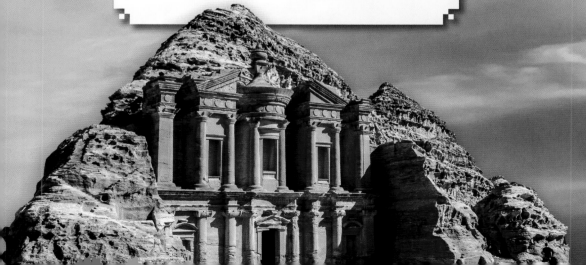

A DESERT TREASURE

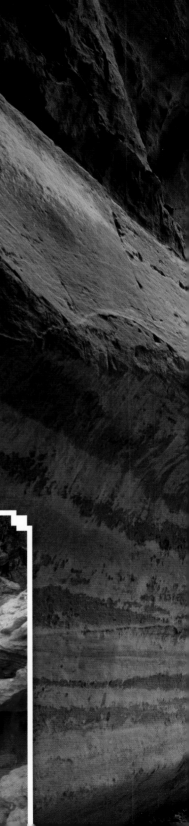

You are on a trip to Jordan, a small country in the **Middle East**. Today, you are visiting the city of Petra. This city in the desert is about three hours from Amman, Jordan's capital city. It is one of the world's largest **archaeological** sites!

Your visit begins with a walk through a canyon path called the Siq. It winds between towering sandstone walls. They are more than 250 feet (76 meters) tall! When you emerge from the Siq, you see a magnificent structure cut from stone. Welcome to Petra!

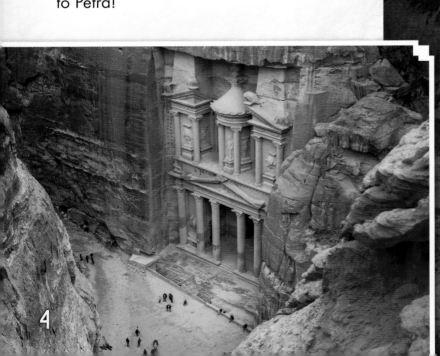

WATER IN THE DESERT

Ancient clay pipelines can be seen on the canyon walls during the walk through the Siq. These clay pipes once brought water down to the center of Petra.

VIEW FROM THE SIQ

WHAT IS PETRA?

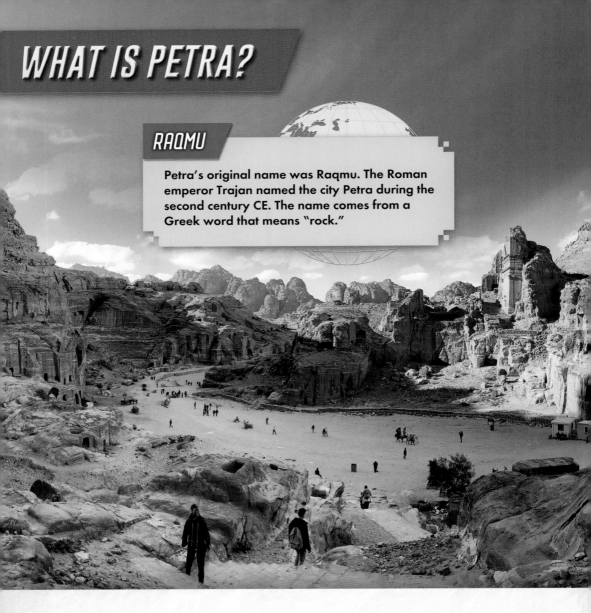

Petra is an ancient desert city carved from sandstone walls. It is in Jordan near the town Wadi Musa. Petra lies in a dry valley surrounded by mountains and canyons. The city spreads out over more than 100 square miles (259 square kilometers) across rocky **terrain**. The sandstone's pinkish color gives Petra the nickname the "Rose City."

Visitors to Petra walk and climb to see structures carved into sandstone. These structures include **tombs** and temples. Some structures have elegant **facades**. Others have simpler designs.

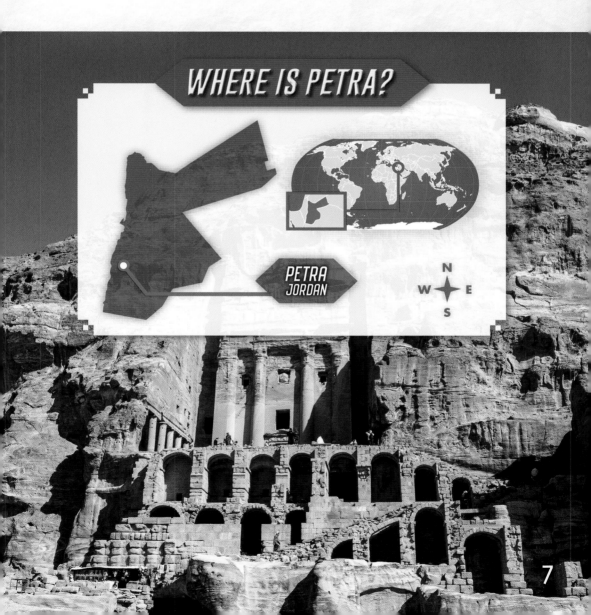

WHERE IS PETRA?

PETRA
JORDAN

N
W E
S

Petra is known for its remarkable **architecture**. The Treasury is over 130 feet (40 meters) tall. It is decorated with elegant columns and carvings. Its name comes from a story about treasure hidden inside it. However, no treasure has ever been found. The structure was likely used as a tomb for a king.

TREASURY

SANDSTONE STAIRWAY

The Monastery is the largest temple in Petra. Visitors must climb 800 steps to get to the top!

MONASTERY

Another famous building is the Monastery. It was most likely used as a temple. The top of the Monastery features a cone-shaped roof topped by an **urn**. Petra's largest freestanding building is the Great Temple. It covers an area more than twice the size of a football field!

GREAT TEMPLE

INNOVATIVE ENGINEERS

The Nabataean people were among the first people to live in Petra. These **nomads** arrived between the 6th and 4th centuries BCE.

CISTERN

The desert landscape made settlement difficult. But the Nabataeans had a solution. They developed a system to capture and store water in **cisterns**. They laid pipes in channels carved through solid rocks. The pipes brought water to Petra from springs 5 miles (8 kilometers) away. The Nabataeans also built dams to capture flood water from winter rains.

DAM

11

Thanks to the water system, Petra became a lush city dotted with gardens, orchards, and fountains. People used the water to drink, bathe, and **irrigate** crops. There were even pools to swim in!

Petra soon became a trading hub. Traders passed through Petra from present-day Asia, Europe, and Africa. The traders carried spices, silk, and many other goods. Travelers found food, water, and lodging in Petra. Petra's location and water supply led it to become the capital of the Nabataean kingdom.

THEN AND NOW

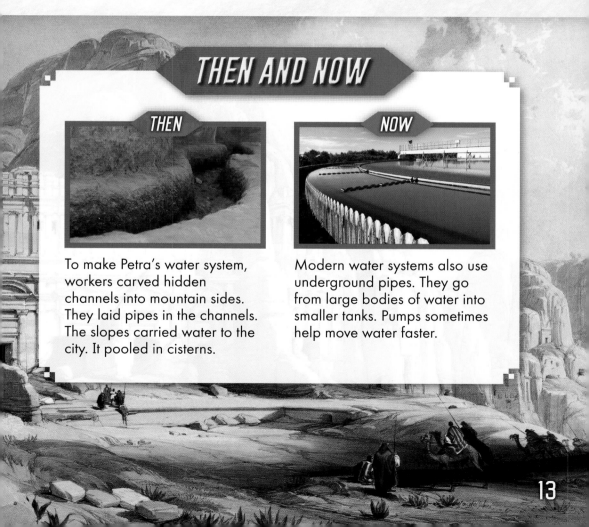

THEN

To make Petra's water system, workers carved hidden channels into mountain sides. They laid pipes in the channels. The slopes carried water to the city. It pooled in cisterns.

NOW

Modern water systems also use underground pipes. They go from large bodies of water into smaller tanks. Pumps sometimes help move water faster.

The water system and trading helped Petra become a wealthy city. The Nabataeans were able to build dozens more buildings. They built temples and fancy houses. They even built theaters. The largest could hold thousands of people!

THINK ABOUT IT

How did Petra's water system help the city gain wealth?

THEATER

A CITY OF RICHES

For about 400 years, Petra was one of the world's wealthiest cities. Its population probably numbered around 25,000 at its peak.

Many of Petra's facades were built between the 1st century BCE and 2nd century CE. The Nabataeans also dug hundreds of caves from the sandstone. More than 800 caves have been identified as tombs.

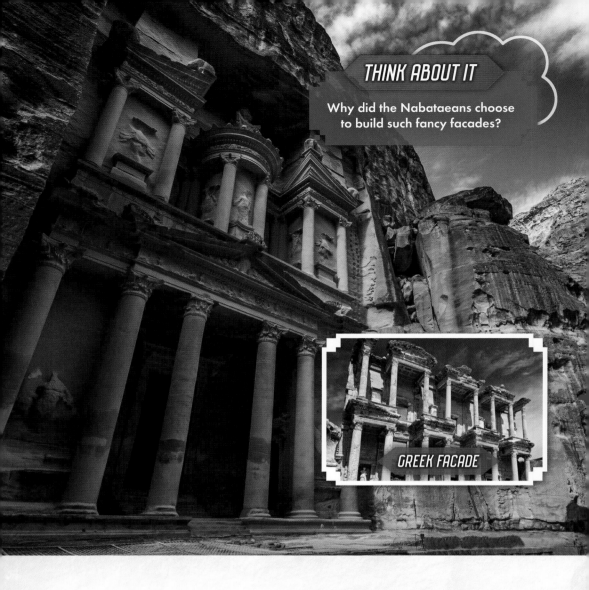

THINK ABOUT IT

Why did the Nabataeans choose to build such fancy facades?

GREEK FACADE

The Nabataeans copied building styles from many regions. For example, the columns at the Great Temple are topped with carvings of Asian elephant heads! The Treasury's facade is similar to some found in ancient Greek buildings.

The Nabataeans were master builders. Workers stood on steps made from planks placed in the rock. They moved from top to bottom to carve the facades with hammers and chisels. The Nabataeans built their freestanding structures from sandstone. The builders cut the stone and dragged it over rollers to move it.

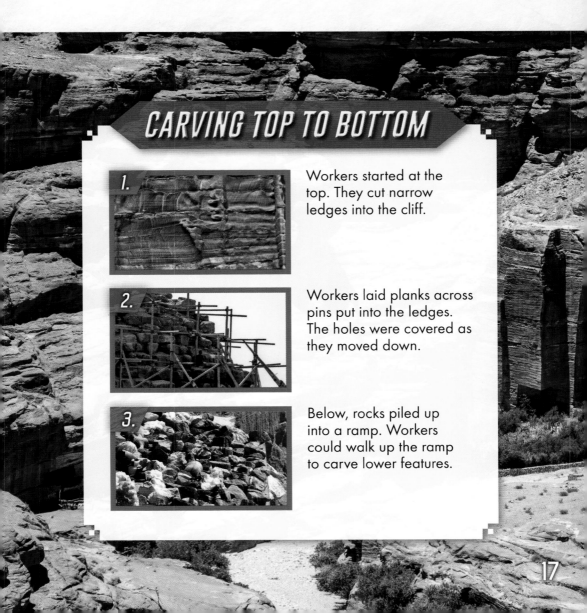

CARVING TOP TO BOTTOM

1. Workers started at the top. They cut narrow ledges into the cliff.

2. Workers laid planks across pins put into the ledges. The holes were covered as they moved down.

3. Below, rocks piled up into a ramp. Workers could walk up the ramp to carve lower features.

EQUAL RIGHTS

Petra did not have slavery. Women and men were given equal rights. Both had roles in politics!

Astronomy and religion may have been important to Petra's builders. Some structures appear to track the movements of the sun, moon, and stars. During the winter **solstice**, the light of the setting sun enters the gate of the Monastery. It lights up stone blocks used as a throne for a Nabataean god.

The rays of the setting sun also light up the rocks opposite the Monastery. An image of a lion's head appears on them. The lion was the symbol for a Nabataean goddess!

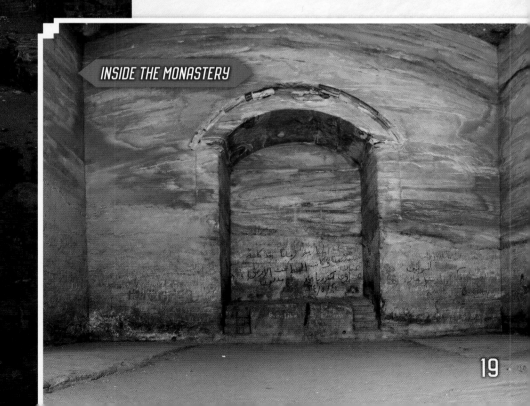

INSIDE THE MONASTERY

LOST AND FOUND

BEAUTIFUL FLOORS

One church in Petra is famous for its floors. They are covered with designs of birds, camels, and other animals!

Petra's wealth eventually attracted the attention of Roman leaders. Rome took control of Petra in 106 CE without a fight. The Romans shifted trade routes to cities further north and to the sea. Over time, Petra lost its status as an important trade center and sank into decline.

More setbacks followed. Major earthquakes in 363 and 551 greatly damaged the city and its water supply system. The population dwindled. In time, Petra fell into ruin.

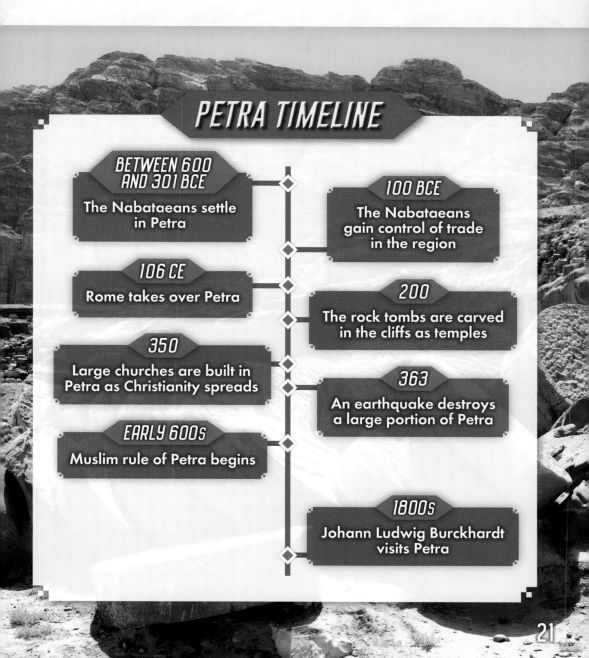

PETRA TIMELINE

BETWEEN 600 AND 301 BCE
The Nabataeans settle in Petra

100 BCE
The Nabataeans gain control of trade in the region

106 CE
Rome takes over Petra

200
The rock tombs are carved in the cliffs as temples

350
Large churches are built in Petra as Christianity spreads

363
An earthquake destroys a large portion of Petra

EARLY 600S
Muslim rule of Petra begins

1800S
Johann Ludwig Burckhardt visits Petra

BEDOUINS

For hundreds of years, western countries had little knowledge about Petra's location. A nomadic group called the Bedouins took over the region and lived in Petra's caves.

In the early 1800s, a Swiss traveler named Johann Ludwig Burckhardt visited Petra. Amazed by Petra's beauty, he revealed its location to others. Soon, western scientists arrived to study and map the city. In 1929, British scientists began the first **excavations** in the city.

JOHANN LUDWIG BURCKHARDT

MODERN EXCAVATION SITE

GREAT TEMPLE
BROWN UNIVERSITY
EXCAVATION

EXPLORE, RESTORE, AND PROTECT

Only a small part of Petra has been uncovered. Even so, researchers have made many important discoveries. These include thousands of **artifacts**, such as Nabataean coins, jewelry, and pieces of statues.

NABATAEAN ARTIFACT

PETRA MUSEUM

PAPYRUS SCROLLS
FOUND IN PETRA

Other finds reveal more clues about life in Petra. Around 150 **papyrus** scrolls were discovered in an excavated church in 1993. These scrolls described parts of everyday life. They showed weddings, sales, and legal records. They are more than 1,000 years old!

Teams are also working to **restore** Petra. Sandstorms and flooding have caused damage from **erosion**. In some places, the stone appears to have melted away!

EROSION ON STAIRS

COMPARE AND CONTRAST

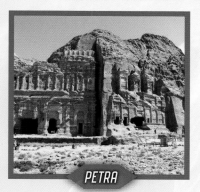

PETRA

MESA VERDE

LOCATION
Jordan

PURPOSE
city for ancient Nabataean people

BUILT
between the 6th and
4th centuries BCE

NOTABLE STRUCTURES
Treasury, Monastery

LOCATION
United States

PURPOSE
city for ancient Pueblo people

BUILT
around 600 CE

NOTABLE STRUCTURES
Cliff Palace

Technology may help scientists find solutions. Scientists use **imaging technology** to understand how the Nabataeans managed water flow. In time, scientists may get the water system working again. They could channel water away from weak areas. Technology also helps scientists make new discoveries. In 2016, scientists used drones and satellite imaging to discover a monument the size of an Olympic swimming pool!

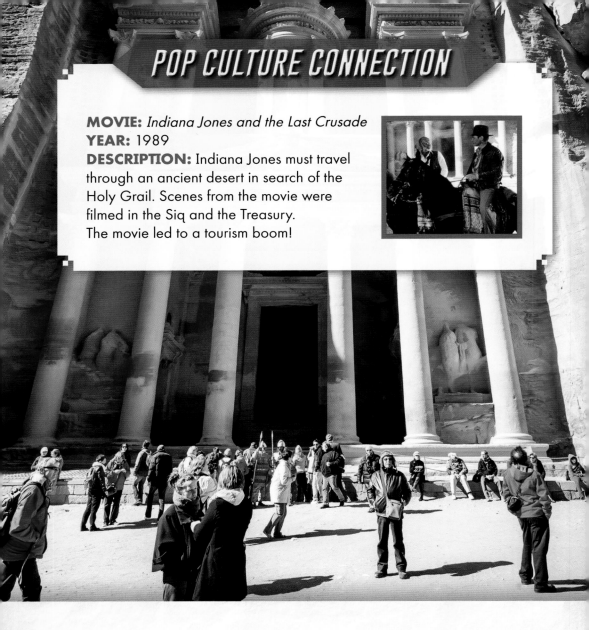

POP CULTURE CONNECTION

MOVIE: *Indiana Jones and the Last Crusade*
YEAR: 1989
DESCRIPTION: Indiana Jones must travel through an ancient desert in search of the Holy Grail. Scenes from the movie were filmed in the Siq and the Treasury. The movie led to a tourism boom!

In 1985, Petra was declared a **UNESCO** World Heritage Site. It drew many visitors. But **tourism** caused some problems. Ancient walls and paths were worn down by thousands of visitors. In 1989, Jordan started the Petra National Trust. Its guidelines for tourism help protect the city.

In 2007, Petra was named a Wonder of the Modern World. It remains Jordan's top attraction. With careful restoration, Petra will remain a wonder for years to come!

PETRA BY NIGHT

Special night tours are held every week in Petra. More than 1,500 candles light the Treasury!

GLOSSARY

archaeological—related to the study of things left behind by ancient people

architecture—the design of buildings

artifacts—items made long ago by humans; artifacts tell people today about people from the past.

cisterns—tanks for storing water

erosion—the process through which rocks are worn away by wind, water, ice, or human activity

excavations—processes in which people dig to discover things

facades—the fronts of buildings

imaging technology—a technology that uses radar to find and take pictures of hidden objects

irrigate—to bring water to crops through human-made channels

Middle East—a region of southwestern Asia and northern Africa; this region includes Egypt, Lebanon, Iran, Iraq, Israel, Saudi Arabia, Syria, and other nearby countries.

nomads—people who have no fixed home but wander from place to place

papyrus—a paperlike material made from plants that was used for writing on

restore—to return something to its original condition

solstice—an event that happens twice a year when the sun reaches its highest or lowest point in the sky

terrain—the physical features of an area

tombs—structures that hold the remains of people who have passed away

tourism—the business of people traveling to visit other places

UNESCO—the United Nations Educational, Scientific and Cultural Organization; UNESCO works to educate people and preserve world landmarks.

urn—a small container used to hold ashes

TO LEARN MORE

AT THE LIBRARY

Jackson, Tom. *Wonders of the World*. New York, N.Y.: DK Publishing, 2014.

Rechner, Amy. *Jordan*. Minneapolis, Minn.: Bellwether Media, 2018.

Wolny, Philip. *What Are Deserts?* New York, N.Y.: The Rosen Publishing Company, 2019.

ON THE WEB

FACTSURFER

Factsurfer.com gives you a safe, fun way to find more information.

1. Go to www.factsurfer.com.

2. Enter "Petra" into the search box and click 🔍.

3. Select your book cover to see a list of related content.

INDEX

architecture, 8
artifacts, 24, 25
astronomy, 19
Bedouins, 22
building styles, 16
Burckhardt, Johann Ludwig, 23
carvings, 6, 7, 8, 11, 16, 17
caves, 15, 22
church, 20, 25
cisterns, 11
compare and contrast, 27
construction, 11, 14, 15, 17
decline, 20, 21
discoveries, 24, 25, 27
equal rights, 18
erosion, 26
excavations, 23, 25
facades, 7, 15, 16, 17
Great Temple, 9, 16
imaging technology, 27
Indiana Jones and the Last
    Crusade, 28
Jordan, 4, 6, 28, 29
location, 4, 6, 7, 13, 22, 23
Monastery, 9, 19

Nabataeans, 10, 11, 13, 14,
    15, 16, 17, 19, 24, 27
name, 6, 8
Petra National Trust, 28
pipes, 5, 11
pop culture connection, 28
population, 15, 21
religion, 19
restore, 26, 29
Rome, 6, 20
sandstone, 4, 6, 7, 15, 17
scrolls, 25
Siq, 4, 5
size, 4, 6, 8, 9
then and now, 13
think about it, 14, 16
timeline, 21
tourism, 28, 29
trading, 13, 14, 20
Treasury, 8, 16, 29
UNESCO, 28
water, 5, 11, 12, 13, 14,
    21, 27

The images in this book are reproduced through the courtesy of: Jan Wlodarczyk/ Alamy, front cover; tenkl, pp. 3, 9 (top), 31; jaras72, p. 4; Thanida Siritan, p. 5; anahtiris, p. 6; Flamingo Eilat, p. 7 (top); volkova natalia, p. 7 (bottom); Yongyut Kumsri, p. 8; ariy, p. 9 (bottom); PhotoStock-Israel/ Alamy, pp. 10, 13 (bottom); Arco Images GmbH/ Alamy, 11 (top), 21, 23 (bottom); agefotostock/ Alamy, p. 11 (bottom); Niday Picture Library/ Alamy, p. 12; Natalia Lukiianova/ Alamy, p. 13 (top); Cindy Hopkins/ Alamy, p. 13 (then); Dmitri Ma, p. 13 (now); angela Meier, p. 14; Ivan NL, p. 15; Kanuman, p. 16 (top); Ian Littlewood/ Alamy, p. 16 (Greek facade); Juliane Thiere/ Alamy, p. 16 (bottom); Frank Heinz/ Alamy, p. 17 (step 1); Thomas Wyness, p. 17 (step 2); paintings, p. 17 (step 3); Igor Dymov/ Alamy, p. 17 (bottom); Punnawit Suwuttananun/ Getty Images, p. 18; Hanis, p. 19; Matyas Rehak, p. 20; NadyaRa, p. 22; Rapp Halour/ Alamy, p. 23 (top); Ilan Amihai/ Alamy, p. 24 (top); Ian Bottle/ Alamy, p. 24 (bottom); Paul and Nancy Lapp Collection. May 1995. ACOR/ American Center of Oriental Research, p. 25; Karol Kozlowski Premium RM Collection/ Alamy, p. 26; Yasemin Olgunoz Berber, p. 27 (Petra); MarclSchauer, p. 27 (Mesa Verde); Alice Dragon/ Alamy, p. 27 (bottom); United Archives GmbH/ Alamy, p. 28 (top); vvoe, p. 28 (bottom); EyesTravelling, p. 29.